# The Death Row Shuffle

poems by

# Howie Good

Finishing Line Press
Georgetown, Kentucky

# The Death Row Shuffle

Copyright © 2020 by Howie Good
ISBN 978-1-64662-287-0 First Edition
All rights reserved under International and Pan-American Copyright Conventions. No part of this book may be reproduced in any manner whatsoever without written permission from the publisher, except in the case of brief quotations embodied in critical articles and reviews.

## ACKNOWLEDGMENTS

The author wishes to thank the editors of the following journals in which some of the poems in this volume originally appeared, occasionally in somewhat different form: *Thimble Literary Magazine; Live Nude Poems; Microfiction Monday; The Big Windows Review: Isacoustic; Dodging the Rain; Boston Literary Magazine: The Voices Project; A Story in 100 Words: Red Eft Review; Biscuit Root Drive; Impaired; All the Sins; misery tourism; What Rough Beast; former people; City. River. Tree.; Club Plum; right hand pointing;* and *As It Ought to Be.*

Publisher: Leah Maines
Editor: Christen Kincaid
Cover Art: johnny_automatic, Courtesy: Open Clip Art Library
Author Photo: Howie Good
Cover Design: Elizabeth Maines McCleavy

Order online: www.finishinglinepress.com
also available on amazon.com

Author inquiries and mail orders:
Finishing Line Press
P. O. Box 1626
Georgetown, Kentucky 40324
U. S. A.

# Table of Contents

The Secret Goldfish .................................................................. 1
In Case of Fire .......................................................................... 2
Oracle ......................................................................................... 3
Heartsick .................................................................................... 4
The End of Nature .................................................................. 5
Birth, Death, Etc. .................................................................... 6
Love in Time of . . . ................................................................. 7
Between Everything and Nothing ...................................... 8
Complicity ................................................................................. 9
American Tune ....................................................................... 10
The Third Reich of Dreams ................................................ 11
Springtime Elegy .................................................................... 12
Threatened Birds Nesting .................................................... 13
That Winter Spring Came Late ......................................... 14
Cold Sun ................................................................................... 15
On Being Rendered Speechless .......................................... 16
The Way to Dusty Death ..................................................... 17
Drive ........................................................................................... 18
Please Scream Inside Your Heart ....................................... 19
Flurries ...................................................................................... 20
A Simple Prayer ...................................................................... 21
Apathy for the Devil .............................................................. 22
The Death Row Shuffle ........................................................ 23
What Makes the Dark So Dark .......................................... 24
Between Life and Death ....................................................... 25
Without a Map ........................................................................ 26
Flight into Darkness .............................................................. 27
Graveyard Shuffle ................................................................... 28
April Come She Will ............................................................. 29
Love Note ................................................................................. 30
The Carnival of Being ........................................................... 31
Sick World ................................................................................ 32

*It's the way we all live.
Shallow life, shallow ditch.
Big life, big abyss.*

—Nick Toshces

**The Secret Goldfish**

My mother during one of her frequent fits flushed my goldfish down the toilet while I was at school. This was long before children had only the water from toilets to drink. I'd won the goldfish at a carnival by somehow tossing a ping-pong ball into the fish's bowl. But awful sights were creeping up on me even then. I have memories of little ballerinas in disintegrating tulle tutus and dance slippers made of bubble wrap and tape. And because I was in the country I was in, there were dim streetlamps at dusk, there were burnt holes for eyes.

**In Case of Fire**

The seamstresses bend to the demanding work of sewing mouths shut with curved needles and fire retardant thread. And why shouldn't they? The only words anyone ever truly needs have all been cannibalized for parts. It's the reason I carry a lot of photos in my phone. Still, if someone announces, "I think I'm going to kill myself," you should take it seriously. I've been lingering for a while now very close to a volcano with a beautiful name.

**Oracle**

A woman named for a dead grandmother crossed her arms across her chest in a conscious attempt to hide her trembling. She thought the birds up in the trees sounded like they were asking, "Hey, you all right?" Most of her communications with the world were strained or superficial. It took awhile before she realized that everything she was interested in saying was contained somewhere in a book. Now when she closes her eyes, she can see flowers, fire creatures, viruses leaping from the cracked tarmac. She hesitates to call them visitors. More like chasing pink, she found red.

**Heartsick**

The doctor is absurdly talkative. "Apparently it's Mental Health Awareness Day today," he says. "And ski season is coming. I've never been to California and, yes, that's sad." He keeps up his chattering while jamming a giant needle into my chest. I beg him, "Stop, stop, please stop." He just pushes the needle in deeper. I'm screaming now. A nurse hurries in. "Almost there," the doctor calmly tells her, referring, I imagine in my distress, to the outskirts of heaven, where angels, some the size of a grain of salt, some the size of a pebble, buzz like dung flies.

**The End of Nature**

I fell asleep to the rat-tat-tat of rain and dreamed I could breathe underwater. The grieving came later, when they cut open the belly of a stranded whale and found coins and plastic water bottles inside. Then I learned there could be such a thing as too much sun. Now I'm wondering what comes next, if we'll only be able to view nature in assigned locations. You'll go and sit in a darkened theater, surrounded by dozens of strangers, and when you start to sob, not even half the people there will understand.

**Birth, Death, Etc.**

Somewhere I have a picture postcard of Kafka's birthplace in Prague. Even the cashiers at the gift shop there were imbued with a kind of perverted charm, offering suggestions about how to be productive while extremely depressed. Linger someplace too long, though, and the infrastructure starts to crumble. I was an adult when I realized there's no word that designates a person as being a parent who has lost a child—a word like "widow" or "orphan." Sartre's last words were, "I failed." Flags were burned in protest. The rest just flung flowers.

**Love in Time of . . .**

The spring has started off all wrong. It's been dark and murky, and I've got no idea why. I'm struggling to keep the screech of panic out of my voice. Chinese! The sky is full of them. I think maybe what I need more than isolation or bleach is the soft, reassuring weight of your body on mine. The grim faces on TV advise completely the opposite, but we're meant to be held by each other, amazed by how much we can touch.

**Between Everything and Nothing**

Some people like shiny things, other people don't. At the beginning, I liked almost nothing. Now I like almost everything. I just keep my eyes open and see what comes. If you surrender to the air, you can ride it. It's not exactly a plan—more a mindset. I think everyone is beautiful, can be beautiful. It's a matter of choice in some way. One day a stranger walked up to me and he said, "I am completely overwhelmed." Get used to it! The symphony in the elevator, the ballet at the bus stop, the tunnels made by the worms.

**Complicity**

We dance with skeletons. We steal cable. We leave violent stains on the carpet. We shift the blame to the fellaheen digging for papyri at an ancient historical site. We cross off career options. We put likeable liars in office and dark-skinned mothers and babies in jail. We go around looking for this or that clue, this or that miraculous city, without even once catching a glimpse. Rather, where our gaze just happens to fall, worse soon follows. The ground bleeds, the moon aches. Fire chews through brick walls. Ideas lose elasticity. The dreaming heads of sleepers get pried open

**American Tune**

Love everything that lives and be fair to all the parts and do not have a hierarchy, but should the uniforms come for you under the cover of night to convey you back across the border, resolve to become like the wind that dies one moment only to return the next as poems and explosions.

&

We were a block or so from our hotel, holding hands like a couple of teenagers, when we saw the dark, lumpy shape, a homeless person wrapped in a shroud of blankets and sleeping on cardboard, but said nothing about it, quick looked away and walked past at a picked-up pace, as if a crime had just been committed and our entire role in it was to forget.

&

You arrive with 100 gallons of red paint, and all these people are thinking, "Oh my God," while you work out the next steps that need to be taken. It kind of gives you something to do with your sadness. You serve an idea that doesn't belong to you. There's no way you can just stop. You've got to keep accelerating. The invisible world is teetering between becoming and dying, and it can go in either direction at any moment. So the answer is "no" should anyone happen to ask if every ray of light comes back to us.

## The Third Reich of Dreams

I dreamed that it was forbidden to dream, but that I did anyway. In the morning the phone rang. A dull voice said, "This is the Monitoring Office." I started begging and pleading that this one time I be forgiven—please just don't report anything this one time, don't pass it on, please just forget it. The voice remained absolutely silent and then hung up. Over the next few days, street signs were replaced on every corner with posters proclaiming, in white letters on a black background, the 20 words people weren't allowed to say. The first was "Lord"; the last was "I."

*Sources: https://neglectedbooks.com/?p=4797; https://www.newyorker.com/books/second-read/how-dreams-change-under-authoritarianism*

**Springtime Elegy**

Spring has been halted for cause. Everything is either too hot or too cold, and nothing is soft. The ancient Chinese would carry lanterns lit by fireflies when passing through the streets at night. All times and places display the same treacheries, tell the same lame lies, just with different words, a cacophony of gods, demons, animals. I have spent too many late hours watching out the window, waiting for something else to happen, for murderous regimes to collapse, for the moon to ooze life, for once-extinct pigeons to come strutting back into view, for these broken branches to very nearly flower.

**Threatened Birds Nesting**

You're eating lunch on a bench in the park, close to a roped-off area where a sign says threatened birds are nesting. It's the first nice day in a week. You're enjoying the spring-like weather when a man you've never seen before steps out from behind a tree. He points a .38 special at you, shouts, "I regard Henry Ford as an inspiration," and fires. Within just hours, friends assemble a pop-up shrine at the spot, with flowers, teddy bears, messages of love and respect. Although not me. I'm reading true crime books in order to gather survival tips.

**That Winter Spring Came Late**

Like yesterday
and the day before,
today will be long,
yet another void to behold,

sunlight reduced
to puzzling remnants,
chalky gray shreds,

and the leaf buds closed
until further notice.

**Parable**

They removed centuries of books
from library shelves, and on a special night

they carted the books to the square
where they had built a bonfire,

and while a large and encouraging crowd
excitedly looked on, they threw the books,

some as thick as a loaf of bread,
others as thin as just a slice, into the fire,

and the book covers curled and wilted,
and the pages turned to clotted ash,

but the words like sparks flew upwards.

**Cold Sun**

Every day the world
burns down anew
on the six o'clock news.

A window shimmering
with streaming raindrops
moves me more,

like the saddest sadness ever,
but cast in platinum
and encased in diamonds.

**On Being Rendered Speechless**

Picking up and dropping off passengers there
is prohibited by law, even when driving a luxury sedan,

so we might as well stay right where we are,
entwined around each other, the bed squeaking

unintelligibly under us as we grunt and gasp,
just about to let go of our entire combined vocabularies,

and all without what the guardians of language
would consider an appropriate level of remorse.

**The Way to Dusty Death**

Ducks are swimming
in Rome's fountains,

dolphins splashing
in Venice's canals.

The loud sun blinds
with cold, slimy energy.

Rudolph Hess, the only
inmate in Spandau Prison,

was 93 years old when
he hanged himself in his cell.

On a train bound for nowhere
you know where you are.

**Drive**

I was driving because
she couldn't drive a stick,
my window half-open,
the air rushing past,
whup-whup-whup,
when suddenly there was
a sulfur smell as of witches
burning. She looked up
from her phone screen
and saw the dreary sky
and a homeless vet on crutches,
then the ramshackle ruins
of an abandoned factory
behind prison fencing.
"Are we lost?" she asked.
Well, yeah, maybe.

**Please Scream Inside Your Heart**

Often these days I don't quite know
where I am, just that wherever I am,
dream, myth, fable, there are admiring statues
of homicidal generals on horseback
and many more of a white Jesus on foot,
and whether it was the Vikings or Columbus
who discovered America is immaterial,
especially as the clouds immediately overhead
resemble bloody scabs and crumpled dollar bills,
and the only advice anyone ever offers is,
if you have to scream, scream silently.

**Flurries**

Small white envelopes
blowing all about,
some torn open
and already empty,
but others with invitations
to a children's party
forever sealed inside

**A Simple Prayer**

My mom went
into the hospital
13 years ago today
and never came out.

Lord, protect me,
so every morning
I can sit by the window
and start a poem.

There's a beauty
in inventing things
that serve no purpose.

**Apathy for the Devil**

This is the country you heard rumors about, where the sky acquires the greenish sheen of sickness and birds are forced by the diseased air to fly close to the ground, where memory lasts just a very short time, where school hallways are spotted with blood and the cops have a penchant for suicide, where deranged angels hoot all night in the tree outside your window, where thought is folly and endings go spectacularly wrong, where love, invisible until now but always there, spreads like a spider crack.

**The Death Row Shuffle**

I felt like I was on a bridge, and there were two or three heavy trucks, and the bridge was rocking—but there were no trucks. Even the dairy cows wondered what the fuck. At one point we seemed to be following Beethoven's footsteps through Vienna. This was someone's idea of paradise. It just wasn't mine. I wore only a sports jacket and shoes, no shirt or pants. The local women said that when the time came, they wanted to be buried in their wedding dresses. They would later tell us many other disturbing things as machine guns swept the streets.

**What Makes the Dark So Dark**

I'm no psychologist, or any other kind of -ologist, but before you go to bed at night, look at the darkness. We're living a life of shadows, of echoes, and with some particles capable of switching between the two. You don't look like you anymore. I'm not there even when I am. At times I resolve to become like the drunks who, sufficiently enraged, can just shrug off the effects of being tasered. Other times what interests me isn't success, but love, how the next person adds onto it without knowing all its nimble and sinister tricks.

**Between Life and Death**

We're always evolving, always about to become something else, always both here and not here. Punk musicians who overdosed in flophouses, and child refugees who died in the camps, and American soldiers killed in Iraq pass each other on the worm-eaten stairs. Maybe if I walk really, really carefully, I can escape notice. People are acting more than just a little crazy. I can't see from this distance who that is writhing on the ground, but whoever it is, they're beating him to death with baseball bats. A woman keeps screaming, "No! No!" God is a joke that nobody gets.

**Flight into Darkness**

I seem to have discovered my shadow side—a wardrobe with mystery contents, blue and purple and full of leprous spots. Which isn't to say I feel sad or lonely. Rather, I'm noticing different details. The world right now, mostly it's news of the virus. We first heard the rumors from travelers. Men: quiet, faces drawn; women: often sobbing. We didn't believe them. The weather was just too beautiful. We lazed around, eating cherries, one basket after another, and ignored the elderly stumbling down the road from time to time, buckling under their loads.

**Without a Map**

That country no longer exists. If you ever go searching for it—in books or on old maps—you'll find only a confusion of names. Yesterday I was walking and walking and walking and writing poetry in my head, and when I looked up, I realized I had no idea where I was. You don't believe something like that is ever going to happen to you. And then it does. The world is just so huge none of us is a hundred percent safe. "Is that vehicle following me?" I find myself wondering. "Are those cameras on that turret trained on me?" Somehow the false expresses what might be real. A hunter thinks he shot a deer when he actually shot his brother.

**Graveyard Shuffle**

We were born in an idiot town, given only clichés to speak, warned by the police not to mix up the words or stray too far from the basic script. Without realizing it, we have been marching to the town cemetery beside our own coffins ever since. Look at these dirty stairs. Look at the darkness pooled at the bottom of them. Then listen to the beat of your blood, and when you do, light will erupt, even if it's just for a minute, and sea nymphs with red seaweed hair will sun themselves on the ledges of seaside cliffs.

**April Come She Will**

Men on the street would call my girlfriend *lindo*. "Get used to it," she said. I decided the best thing for me to do was nothing. April had been designated Artichoke Month. I remember we saw a movie about astronauts on a mind-bending journey to the cosmic womb. It was confusing and a little scary. She got really into a singer-songwriter who had committed suicide by stabbing himself in the chest. There were long lines outside liquor stores and gun shops. One day we found a crudely lettered cardboard sign lying abandoned on the sidewalk: Hungry & Cold / Anything Helps.

**Love Note**

Even though the sign says, "Do not swim near seals," we'll have fun, go on a picnic in the hills, maybe spend the whole night there, so many stars that the sky looks perforated by cosmic buckshot, or we'll sleep in and then helicopter over traffic jams, moving, breathing, shining from rehab center to wedding cake palace, while the angel of death rolls a cigarette and the border wall sinks another quarter of an inch, and this will happen again and again, people turning up at all hours to complain bitterly about being written out of our story.

## The Carnival of Being

It's so bleak outside I decide to hide out for the day in my little room. The other first-floor tenant has removed his clothes and walked off down the street. I can't stop replaying in my head the saddest sound in the world, a shovelful of soil thumping the lid of a coffin. For now, at least, there's no great difference between a funeral and a carnival. Volunteer firefighters have been going about the neighborhood distributing oxygen masks for pets. Asthma sufferers, especially. That's the problem with people who put Velveeta on enchiladas; they can't tell anymore what's appropriate. By evening, white hairs have sprouted on just one side of my moustache.

**Sick World**

A usually bustling city is eerily vacant. Essential supplies now include liquor, guns, and toilet paper. Who isn't secretly embarrassed? Around midnight I take a puzzle apart just for the hell of it. The next morning my department holds a Zoom session on how to prevent cheating in online classes. Other professors mention they also have been having strange dreams. In mine, I'm eating Crown Fried Chicken on a bench while eyeballs the size of boulders roll across the grass and dirt and a woman I recognize from TV weeps into her hands.

**Howie Good**, Ph.D., a journalism professor at SUNY New Paltz, is the winner of the 2019 Grey Book Press Chapbook Competition for *What It Is and How to Use It*, the 2017 Lorien Poetry Prize from Thoughtcrime Press for *The Loser's Guide to Street Fighting*, and the 2015 Press Americana Prize for Poetry for *Dangerous Acts Starring Unstable Elements*. He co-edits the journals *UnLost* and *Unbroken*.

www.ingramcontent.com/pod-product-compliance
Lightning Source LLC
LaVergne TN
LVHW041557070426
835507LV00011B/1150